W9-AOM-862

Ins**I**de
Government

☆ CONGRESSIONAL ☆
COMMITTEES
☆ ☆

Cass R. Sandak

T F
C B

Twenty-First Century Books
☆ ☆
A Division of Henry Holt and Company
New York

Twenty-First Century Books
A Division of Henry Holt and Company, Inc.
115 West 18th Street
New York, NY 10011

Henry Holt® and colophon are trademarks of
Henry Holt and Company, Inc.
Publishers since 1866

Text copyright © 1995 by Cass R. Sandak
All rights reserved.
Published in Canada by Fitzhenry & Whiteside Ltd.
195 Allstate Parkway, Markham, Ontario L3R 4T8

Library of Congress Cataloging-in-Publication Data
Sandak, Cass R.
Congressional committees / Cass R. Sandak. — 1st ed.
p. cm. — (Inside government)
Includes bibliographical references (p.) and index.
1. United States. Congress—Committees—Juvenile literature. I. Title. II. Series.
JK1029.S35 1995
328.73'0765—dc20   95–19448
CIP
AC
ISBN 0–8050–3425–0
First Edition 1995

Designed by Kelly Soong

Printed in Mexico
All first editions are printed on acid-free paper ∞.
10 9 8 7 6 5 4 3 2 1

Photo Credits

pp. 8, 11, 14, 31, 42: The Bettmann Archive; pp. 9, 20, 30, 46, 50: AP/Wide World
Photos

CONTENTS

COMMITTEES MAKE HEADLINES

PLAUDITS DROWN OUT CRITICS AS SENATE CONFIRMS BREYER
(from the *New York Times*, July 30, 1994)

SENATE PASSES 5% ARTS CUT
(from the *New York Times*, July 27, 1994)

COMMITTEES, LOBBYISTS AND THE HEALTH REFORM ISSUE
(from the *New York Times*, July 6, 1994)

A DEFEAT ON THE CRIME BILL SHAKES CLINTON: COULD GRIDLOCK
RETURN TO A CONGRESS DOMINATED BY DEMOCRATS?
(from *Time* magazine, August 22, 1994)

WHITEWATER HEARING BEGINS BEFORE HOUSE COMMITTEE
(from the *New York Times*, July 27, 1994)

In the summer of 1994, these five issues made daily headlines in newspapers and magazines across the country. The subjects sparked countless editorials and lively discussions everywhere, as well as hours of news coverage. Every one of them was linked to the actions of a congressional committee. Without congressional committees, none of these major news events would have taken place.

The fact is that almost every action our government takes, from the passage of a new law to a refinement in the tax code to a decision on what armaments to build, is first scrutinized and debated in congressional committees. It is only after the various committees have drafted bills, debated their good and bad points, and recommended passage that a bill can continue along the process of being made into a law.

Committees are the place where the real work of government is performed. Almost thirty years before he became president, Woodrow Wilson wrote in his 1885 book, *Congressional Government*, "Congress, in its committee rooms, is Congress at work."[1]

Why does our Congress have committees? And why do we need them?

These and other questions will be answered as this book shows how congressional committees perform their tasks. The story of congressional committees gives an inside look at the way our government really works.

ONE

HOW THE COMMITTEE
SYSTEM DEVELOPED

THE MAKINGS AND WORKINGS OF CONGRESS

In order to understand what committees are and how they work, it is necessary to go back in history and find out about the early days of our government. When the plans for the U.S. government were established in the Constitution, power was divided among the president (or executive branch), the Congress (or legislative branch), and the Supreme Court (or judicial branch). All three branches were—and still are—needed to provide for the balanced running of a democracy for all the country's citizens.

The Constitution provides that "all legislative Powers herein granted shall be vested in a Congress of the United States, which shall consist of a Senate and House of Representatives" (Article I, Section 1). In other words, Congress—consisting of two chambers—is responsible for making our laws. Members of Congress do this by preparing all the bills that may eventually become our laws.

In Article I, Section 7, the Constitution details the procedures Congress uses to initiate, pass, and enact bills. The document that outlines our way of government gives both houses of Congress the right to originate legislation. Once a bill has been approved by Congress, it must be approved by the president before it becomes law.

Only the House may originate bills having to do with money. The writers of the Constitution apparently assumed that representatives—members of Congress's larger house—were more in touch with the values, lifestyles, and desires of the com-

☆ ════════ ☆

*The first Senate session in New York in 1789 was a
bit like an informal gathering compared to a session today.*

mon people. As well, House members were elected directly by
the people, whereas in earlier times senators were appointed.

The Senate has an additional function of advising on and
consenting to treaties. Another Senate charge is examining and
approving certain nominations made by the president (for
example, Supreme Court nominees). In this way, a system of
checks and balances was set up so that no one branch of the
government could assume too much power.

The Senate, with only one hundred members (two from
each state) is sometimes known as the upper house. Senators
serve longer terms—six years, in contrast to representatives, who
are elected for two-year terms. Because there are fewer senators
and they serve longer terms, senators have slightly more prestige
than members of the House. The House of Representatives,

NUMBERING OF CONGRESSES

The first Congress ran from 1789 to March 1791. In January 1995, the 104th Congress commenced, with new members who had been elected in November 1994. A Congress lasts two years and is divided into two sessions. The first year is called the first session and the second year is called the second session. Members of the House of Representatives are elected every two years. However, Senate terms run for six years. Every two years, one-third of the seats in the Senate come up for reelection, so that there is some continuity in the membership in the upper house.

with 435 members drawn proportionately from all the states, is seen by some to be less exclusive than the Senate and is sometimes called the lower house.

The congressional committee system, even though it was never described in the Constitution, is a direct outgrowth of our constitutional plan of representative government. Committees allow legislators to concentrate their energies in their areas of expertise by freeing members of Congress from the responsi-

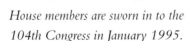

House members are sworn in to the
104th Congress in January 1995.

bility of knowing everything about every matter that comes before them.

The system also provides for a division of labor within the legislative branch. Those representatives and senators who are best qualified to handle certain types of problems are the same ones who evaluate and make recommendations regarding laws that cover these problem areas. In large measure, committee members make up Congress's mind regarding the issues that come before that committee. This takes place because members of Congress tend to listen to one another carefully and take seriously the findings and recommendations of committee members when they report on proposed laws in full session.

Our legislative process helps safeguard our democratic way of life. The system ensures that minority voices are heard in an attempt to meet everyone's needs—not just those of the majority.

HOW COMMITTEES CAME ABOUT

In the beginning, the House of Representatives' first order of business after convening on March 4, 1789, in New York City (then the nation's capital) was to set up Congress's first committee. This committee would lay down the ground rules for conducting legislative business. The fear was that without some kind of guideline, the floor of Congress would soon turn into a free-for-all.

In the country's earliest days, most issues were decided by all senators and representatives in full session. Those were simpler times. The number of players was small and the number of issues coming before Congress was limited. It was still possible to include everyone in every discussion of new policies and laws. Occasionally committees were established as needed so that small numbers of congress members could study and debate particular problems before the whole Congress needed to get involved.

But soon the country began to grow larger, and the country's needs changed. The committee system was established in the House when members realized there was no way everyone could be informed about every issue.

A House committee conducted the first congressional investigation in 1792. The committee wanted to determine whether an army officer had been negligent in allowing some 600 of his soldiers to be killed by Indians in Ohio earlier that year. The general, Major General Arthur St. Clair, had been sent by President George Washington to subdue Indians who had been preventing settlement in the Northwest Territory. During the rout, St. Clair had allowed the deaths of too many militiamen.

☆ ══════ ☆

In the case of Major General Arthur St. Clair (1736–1818) in 1792, Congress assumed the power to investigate in any section of the government.

The committee's findings were inconclusive, but their action set the precedent for every later congressional investigation. The committee established the pattern of Congress assuming responsibility for monitoring the activities of other parts of the U.S. government.

In the Third Congress, which ran from 1793 to 1795, the House set up 350 ad hoc committees—special committees to deal with each piece of legislation that came up for consideration. These special or select (ad hoc) committees had the job of drafting and presenting legislation for voting by Congress in full session.

This meant that each bill (or written idea for a law) had a specific committee assigned to it. Of course, members of all of these committees were drawn from the same small pool of senators and representatives, so each member of Congress had to serve on many different committees. Having so many committees proved unwieldy. Too much time was spent merely on procedural and scheduling concerns. Not enough energy could be devoted to the real work of government—proposing, considering, debating, and passing pieces of legislation.

After each bill was introduced in the House, the Speaker farmed it out to a committee for study. The members of the committee would then report back to the House on whether or not they recommended passage of the measure. In this way, a system developed that relied heavily on committee reports and recommendations. Members of Congress today rely just as heavily on what their colleagues think. The Senate followed the lead established by the House and within a few years set up its own committee structure for dealing with proposed legislation.

THE COUNTRY GROWS

Throughout our nation's history, there has been a constant rise and fall in the number of congressional committees. With more than 350 House committees, it soon became impossible to keep track of the committees, let alone the legislation they were meant to consider. In the early days, as well, our two-party political system had not yet developed; legislators, therefore, had not yet gotten bogged down in political agendas—voting for or against a bill because it supported or undermined the party's position. Partisan differences were developing between those who favored a strong central national government and those who felt that state governments should have more power.

In the early 1800s, the House members agreed to divide the legislative workload among several standing (permanent) committees. By 1795 both the Interstate and Foreign Commerce Committee and the Ways and Means Committee had been established. By 1802 Ways and Means, which sat for discussions of taxation and revenue, had become a standing committee.[1] With the same groups of congressmen considering all the legislative proposals of a certain type, the business of Congress could be somewhat simplified. But after a time, the number of committees again began to grow.

Before the War of 1812, the Senate had just temporary committees. Only the most powerful senators sat on these committees. In 1816 the Senate set up its first permanent committees. There were twelve, of which the Senate Foreign Relations, Finance, and Judiciary Committees have kept their names—and their prestige—to the present day, although some of their responsibilities have changed over the years.

By 1825 the United States government had been in operation for more than thirty-five years. As a result of experience, a more workable plan was put into effect: members of the House and Senate were variously assigned to forty-three different standing, or permanent, committees. Each of these committees had authority over a carefully defined area.

Around the middle of the nineteenth century, it became clear that many committees had no business to conduct. They were, however, listed on official registers. One of the abuses of public officeholders was political patronage. Members of Congress would hand out staff positions for these committees to office seekers as political plums—no-work, no-show type positions that could nonetheless prove lucrative. These positions became sources of bribes to support political patronage.

REFORM

Reform in the Senate in the 1880s changed the rules. Before that time, the system of patronage and rampant political corruption had existed. But reform did not change much. The chairmen of the Senate's many committees—especially those in charge of finance and appropriations—were the most powerful men in Congress. Senators who went along with those in power did well in committee assignments and in other assignments, but those who favored reform were given obscure assignments and often saw their careers languish.

Senator Robert M. La Follette of Wisconsin was a strong believer in the committee system. He was, however, one of the few people who could not accept the way Congress ran itself. Senators were dismayed by his reforming tendencies and sought to diminish La Follette's effectiveness by placing him on virtually powerless committees, such as the Potomac Riverfront Committee. On occasion La Follette would show up at scheduled committee meetings only to be greeted by an empty conference room.

Robert M. La Follette (1855–1925) was an innovator and a spirited politician. He is shown there in the "first radio campaign speech."

Through the end of the nineteenth and beginning of the twentieth centuries, committees seemed to grow and grow. By 1913 the Senate commanded 135 standing committees, and the House was not far behind with 81.

Following World War II, the number of standing committees was cut by more than half. This held true in both the House and Senate. It was all part of the Legislative Reorganization Act of 1946. The act reduced the number of committees in the House to 19 and those in the Senate to 15. Just prior to the 1946 act, the House maintained 48 standing committees; the much smaller Senate had 33. The impetus for change came from two main factors. World War II was over and Congress could once again turn attention to the country's own needs. A new president, Harry S. Truman, was in office, and he believed in simplicity and in streamlining government.

The 1946 act also laid down rules for regularly scheduling committee meetings on specific days and for keeping careful records of votes during committee meetings. The act required committees to have a majority of members present in order to conduct business and to put an end to committee secrecy. It required committee hearings to be opened up to the public, except in cases where national security might be at stake.

But government has a way of becoming bigger and more complex. The tendency toward more complex committees—and greater numbers of them—again asserted itself. By 1970 both chambers had a total count of more than 300 committees and subcommittees. Again the number was reduced in 1976, but by the late twentieth century the work has become so complex and the rules so hard to follow that Congress at large employs a staff of seven full-time parliamentarians (experts in the rules and usages of Congress) as well as a legal assistant, clerk, and secretary just to keep procedural issues in line. Even today, Congress may find that desired legislation has been defeated because of the delaying tactics usually employed by members of the political party opposed to the party that initiated the bill.

TWO

KINDS OF
COMMITTEES

Committees do the work of preparing legislation that is to go before Congress. Nearly every bill is first referred to a committee—only a small number of proposals are acted upon immediately by Congress in full session. The decision to declare war would be one such case. Action cannot be taken on a bill until the appropriate committee has reported on it for floor examination and consideration. The system of referring bills (proposed legislation) to committees for consideration gives ample opportunity for all sides to be heard and to make their views known. Committees, with their structure for listening to testimony and gathering information on all aspects of an issue, provide an open forum for discussion.

Discussion permits a bill to be changed, or amended, before it is signed into law, and full opportunity is given for a bad proposal to be defeated. The damage done by passage of a bad law may take generations to try to correct—for example, the decision by Congress during World War II to intern citizens of Japanese origin.

We have seen that the committee system was developed by Congress as an orderly way for its members to consider the multifaceted business that arises. But committees can also impede the work of Congress. Committee meetings can so delay action or muddy the waters that simple, swift, decisive action often cannot be taken.

The health care reform proposals introduced by the Clinton administration in the early summer of 1994, toward the end of the 103d Congress's second session, met such a fate. Republicans opposed to the bill raised arguments and counterproposals that put off a vote on the bill, which would have passed into law had a vote been taken in the Congress, which was then dominated by members of the Democratic Party. However, after the November 1994 elections, it became clear that the new Congress would have a Republican majority. Thus the original bill proposed by the Democrats has no further prospects. When and if the issue of health care reform is again addressed, the terms of the proposal will have to be substantially different.

PERMANENT (STANDING) COMMITTEES

The Senate and the House of Representatives each have certain permanent committees, also known as standing committees. Permanent committees are the chief resting place of power in Congress. It is no coincidence that many committees in both houses have overlapping titles and responsibilities. It is another example of how government allows checks and balances in an effort to provide a fair voice for all citizens.

Both Democrats and Republicans in Congress may nominate members for standing committees, but most members of a committee come from the majority party (i.e., the party in power—or the one with the most seats and, therefore, the most members in Congress). Membership on the permanent, or standing, committees is set at the beginning of each congressional session. House membership may shift every two years. But for a senator, the committee assignment may stretch through the entire term of six years—that is, through three full Congresses. Most standing committees range in size between thirty and forty-five members.

One of the ways committees differ is in their jurisdiction—the subject areas of the laws that come under their control. Standing committees vary widely in the subject areas that come under their purview. Some are highly specialized and have agendas that are narrowly defined. The Veterans' Affairs Committees (both houses) and the Small Business Committee (House only) are just two examples.

On the other hand, some committees are very broad based. They represent far-flung empires of influence. For example, the Senate Commerce, Science, and Transportation Committee covers both space and transportation issues as well as the merchant marine, sports, and consumer protection, among other issues.

In general, the broader the jurisdiction of a committee, the more areas of life it touches upon. And the committees that influence the most areas of national life—both of the government and of its citizens—also have the most power.

SELECT COMMITTEES

Each chamber also has select (also known as special, temporary, or ad hoc) committees. These committees are formed to look at new proposals that may not yet have been formulated and presented as bills, to consider alternatives, and to suggest compromise positions over disputed aspects of legislation. Select committees are formed for a special project and usually function for a limited period of time. These committees also conduct investigations and consider broad policy issues. They do not normally consider pending legislation. Some of the more common select committees include the Special Committee on Aging and the Select Committee on Ethics. Other select committees deal with such subjects as Indian affairs and national security.

SUBCOMMITTEES

Because so many standing and select committees cover such broad areas of congressional business, they are broken down even further into numerous subcommittees. Subcommittees are small, generally with two dozen to three dozen members. They are designated to deal with policy issues of limited scope that fall under the umbrella of their parent committee's jurisdiction.

For example, individual subcommittees on Water Resources and Nuclear Regulation (among others) are parts of the Senate Committee on Environment and Public Works. Similarly, the House Committee on Education and Labor has subcommittees devoted to such topics as Labor Management Relations and Elementary, Secondary, and Vocational Education.

The House Budget Committee, set up by the Congressional Budget Act of 1976, has no subcommittees, according to its charter legislation. But it, too, is further divided into smaller committees, which it calls "task forces." These groups investigate specific problems or proposals, for example, how much revenue could be raised by a certain new tax. Another example might be the feasibility of financing a costly new weapons program within current defense guidelines. These groups are really subcommittees, but calling them task forces at least does not violate the terms of the budget act.

The larger, broader committees generally serve as clearinghouses for channeling the flow of congressional business into the appropriate subcommittees, where the first basic examination of potential legislation gets done.

In 1981 there were more than 150 subcommittees in the House and just over 100 in the Senate. For example, the Senate Committee on Banking, Housing, and Urban Affairs has subcommittees that investigate the mortgage and lending industries, housing, the stock market, and other issues.

More and more bills are proposed each year. The total currently ranges between 15,000 and 20,000. The vast majority of them "die" in subcommittee. They die a natural death, usually because of lack of interest. Early in the process, the subcommittee holds a hearing on each piece of legislation that appears promising. The screening work accomplished by subcommittees filters out most of these proposed bits of legislation before they are considered by full committee.

The bill's sponsor speaks in favor of the bill's passage, while the sponsor's colleagues subject the bill to a hearing, much like the legal proceedings that precede a courtroom case. Sub-committee members listen to the arguments and opinions advanced not only by the bill's sponsor or sponsors but by other witnesses, who may include other congress members, concerned citizens, experts in the area affected by the proposed law, lobbyists, et cetera. During this initial airing, the bill either gains

☆ ══════ ☆

First Lady Hillary Rodham Clinton and Ira Magaziner, a White House senior adviser, met with the Senate Finance Committee in 1993 to discuss issues in the health care proposals.

supporters or it doesn't. If it doesn't, the process goes no further. If it does gain support, however, something called a markup session will take place. Members of the subcommittee will literally mark up the bill with recommended changes. This is one of the first steps in turning a bill into a law.

A subcommittee holds hearings and then votes. If the sub-committee approves the bill, it goes to full committee. The process is a painfully slow one that may require endless small and large revisions and word changes.

SENATE COMMITTEES

The Senate chambers are usually not full, except when a vote is due. This is because most of the time senators are off working in small rooms—conference rooms and committee chambers. In these rooms, they are listening to testimony and conducting investigations to see if the bills they are developing are the right ones to become law.

The public may attend these meetings, unless confidential matters are being discussed. For example, operations by a secret organization such as the Central Intelligence Agency (CIA) would never be aired in front of the public.

Among many other tasks, the Senate majority leader needs to monitor the work of Senate committees. There are sixteen standing committees and various subcommittees concerning major policy areas, such as finance, appropriations, government operations, and foreign relations. (See chart in appendix.) The Senate Foreign Relations Committee is very powerful because of its members' special responsibilities to oversee foreign affairs and treaties. Senate leaders appoint committee members from among their party associates. Each committee has a staff as well as its own budget.

HOUSE COMMITTEES

House committees are more numerous than Senate committees. The overwhelming majority of bills originate in the House of Representatives. The House initiates revenue bills—one of its exclusive powers granted by the Constitution. Some of the major House committees are Ways and Means, Appropriations, and Rules. (See chapter 5.) Committees in the House prepare the House agenda, draft bills for consideration, and regulate House procedure. Each committee is controlled by the majority party.

Because the House has more members than the Senate, it has more committees and subcommittees. There are twenty-two standing committees in the House organized around policy areas, and each has its own staff, budget, and subcommittees. (See chart in appendix.)

JOINT COMMITTEES

Congress also has joint committees—ones that include members from both the House and Senate. These may be either permanent committees or ad hoc committees with a single, specific purpose. An example of a joint standing committee is the Joint Committee on Taxation. There are also commissions and boards, which are other types of joint committees. There are also joint partisan, or party, committees. These committees develop programs, publish policy reports, and keep voting records. One aspect of party politics is that each party tries to take credit for any positive measures that are passed and tries to fix the blame on the other party when things go less favorably.

CONFERENCE COMMITTEES

Conference committees are special temporary joint committees involving members of both the Senate and the House of Representatives. In many instances the versions of a particular piece of legislation differ from house to house. These differences—even minor ones—must be hammered out so that both House and Senate approve the same bill. This can be done informally, by staff members who represent members of the corresponding House and Senate committees meeting to reconcile differences in wording and content. This is one way that staff members—nonelected officials who assist senators and representatives—work behind the scenes. Or each house may act on the bill as it was approved in the other house. Or a conference committee can be set up. This happens in the case of roughly 10 percent of the bills that become laws.

The types of disagreements most often concern the details of proposed laws. Through the process of negotiation, members of the temporary conference committee try to develop a compromise position on which both the House and the Senate can agree. The compromise bills that are sent for voting in both the houses must be identical.

The Speaker chooses House members of a conference committee. Senate members are recommended by the majority and minority leaders of the Senate. Often the conference committees work in small meeting rooms to discourage the press and lobbyists from being present. A special room has been set aside in the Capitol where conference committees often meet—on neutral ground. Often there is some jealousy and antagonism among the House and Senate members of a conference committee. Haggling can go on for weeks, as during the 1981 conference committee attempting to finalize President Reagan's tax package. A provision of the bill—a tax credit for owners of wood-burning stoves—that had been passed in the Senate was dropped as a compromise during the conference committee's deliberations.[1]

COMMITTEES
AT WORK

The two essential pieces of work that congressional committees do are (1) considering and passing along pieces of proposed legislation and (2) conducting hearings of an investigative nature.

The activities of some committees—those involved in foreign policy, commerce, and the judiciary—are of consistently greater interest to the public than the workings of most other committees. These important committees touch upon domestic and foreign policy, the prosperity of the nation, and international relations.

Sometimes congressional committees draft bills that are the outcome of studies and hearings that may have lasted a year or more. Particularly complex have been their recommendations to pass laws relating to the armed forces. The Armed Services Committees have to consider, for example, major new weapons programs, the deployment of troops abroad, foreign policy issues as they impact defense programs, military procurement practices, benefits programs for armed services personnel, and the maintenance of specific military installations around the world. Many of these bills, as well as bills covering other broad areas, have each taken several years to prepare.

Congress employs four main forms of introducing a proposal. By far the most common is the bill. Another method is the joint resolution. This is merely a formal statement of position that has been approved in both the House and the Senate. For example, the decision to award the Medal of Honor or to designate a national day of mourning for a famous person might be passed by joint resolution.

Also used occasionally are the concurrent resolution and the simple resolution, both of which are rare, limited in scope, and generally concerned with procedural matters within Congress itself. For example, a concurrent resolution might be passed by each chamber of Congress at the same time to present the outline for a new health policy by a certain date. A simple resolution might be a decision passed unilaterally in either house to take action on an issue by a certain time.

BILLS IN COMMITTEE

In committee a bill is given the most intense scrutiny and consideration by committee members. People ranging from expert witnesses to members of the public are given the opportunity to share their views and concerns. As Donald Ritchie writes in *The Senate*, "Once in Committee, the bill must compete with other measures for a place on the Committee's agenda. Many bills die because they receive no committee attention. If the committee schedules the bill, it may assign it to a subcommittee—a portion of the committee with a specific area of jurisdiction."[1]

In both houses, nearly every bill appears before a standing committee for initial action. There are then four basic paths the committee can take: (1) The committee may report, or recommend passage. This means that it passes along the bill, unchanged, to be voted upon. This rarely happens. (2) Or the committee may report with changes to the proposal. This is what happens most frequently. (3) Or the committee may rewrite the bill entirely. (4) Finally, the committee can kill a piece of legislation by refusing to act upon it at all. This is what is known as pigeonholing, or shelving, a bill. This means putting off action on the bill indefinitely. Chances are the issue will never be acted upon unless another bill is introduced someday that makes the same or a similar proposal.

There are occasions when debate and voting move directly to the full House immediately or after brief committee consideration or when bills have not first been considered by a committee, but these are rare instances. Such exceptions to the rule most often take place during a national crisis, when there is little time for lengthy deliberation.

After consideration, a bill is presented by committee before the actual vote—this is called reporting the bill. The public, the press, and senators and representatives can then get a sense of whether or not the bill will pass.

HOW A BILL IS INTRODUCED

1. A member of Congress may introduce a bill that he or she has originated. Often this bill stems from a promise made during the member's election campaign.

2. The bill may have been drafted by that member's constituents, either individually or as part of an interest group's or a lobby's campaign for particular legislation. One member of Congress, however, must formally present the bill for legislative consideration.

3. The president may introduce a bill by means of executive communication. This is generally a letter from the president, from a member of the president's cabinet, or from an executive agency head, addressed to both the Speaker of the House *and* the president of the Senate (the vice president). The Speaker or the Senate president will formally introduce the proposal, which is then channeled to the appropriate committee for preliminary consideration.

In recent decades, most bills that have eventually passed into law have originated in the executive branch. The executive branch includes not just the president but also cabinet members and any of the federal administrative agencies, as well as law enforcement agencies. After being introduced by executive communication, the proposal is then referred to the standing committee that has jurisdiction over the area of the proposed legislation.

The chairperson of the particular committee is usually the one who formally introduces the bill—either in its original form or with changes he or she may consider desirable. Occasionally, although rarely, an executive communication may be considered by the committee or one of the subcommittees without later being introduced. But very rarely does a committee decide not to introduce such a bill. Most rejections of this type occur only after careful consideration.

IN THE COMMITTEE ROOM

The committee room is set up something like a courtroom. Committee members are seated on a raised platform, or dais, at a large table shaped like a horseshoe. Witnesses testify from a large rectangular table facing the dais and slightly below it.

Party politics plays a big role in committee life. Party members sit together in the committee rooms. Since members of the rival Democratic and Republican parties often find themselves on opposite sides of an issue, this is usually a springboard to debate.

While a bill is in committee, it is examined in minute detail. In debate—an orderly process of argumentation—members of Congress with opposing viewpoints try to establish the good and bad features of the proposed law. Opposition party members may try to discredit the bill, using any means possible. When facts will not work, representatives and senators may resort to rhetoric (fancy language), half-truths, and even nonissues in order to stall a bill that might—if passed—reflect favorably on the opposition party. The opposition party may also try to cast the bill in a bad light to garner grassroots opposition to the bill. This is one of the least attractive faces of politics.

Political maneuverings and side steps are able to delay or even derail passage of needed laws. The result of this posturing is that the work of Congress cannot go forward. This stalemate is often referred to as political gridlock.

After weeks and possibly months of consideration, discussion, and debate, the bill is then reported, or presented for vote, before the full House or Senate. What takes place when legislators vote on the floor of the House or Senate is merely putting a stamp of approval on a document that has been hammered out during months of hard work by committee members.

There are ways to change a bill to make it acceptable to all sides. A compromise may occur, a give-and-take situation where each side comes to accept some terms while giving in on others. Or there may be a reciprocity agreement, which means that if a committee agrees to push one bill through, it is in turn obligated to vote positively for another issue that is coming up.

In the struggle over a particular piece of legislation, a coalition sometimes forms, bringing together members of Congress from essentially different groups. In spite of their different parties or different sides on an issue, individuals may come to agree on a plan of action for resolution of a particular issue.

Sometimes various caucuses join together to form the coalition. A caucus is a group made up of members with like-minded political goals that exists within the legislature. For example, there is a women's caucus, a Democratic caucus, a black caucus, and an antiabortion caucus.

Committees ultimately decide the fate of proposed legislation. Most bills are effectively killed in committees. Of the other proposed changes to laws, some are rewritten and some are approved. For example, in the Ninety-Ninth Congress (from 1984 to 1986) there were 11,602 pieces of legislation considered in Congress, with 7,522 coming from the House and 4,080 introduced in the Senate. Of these, only 664 bills were enacted as law, which amounts to less than 6 percent of those bills that were started.

CHRISTMAS TREES AND COOKIE JARS

Some bills are known as Christmas tree bills. Members of Congress demand additions and changes to the bill in much the same way they would hang ornaments on a holiday tree. Other bills are known as cookie jar bills, because they hold goodies for everyone.

COMMITTEE HEARINGS (INVESTIGATIONS)

One of the principal ways congressional investigating committees collect information is by calling witnesses and collecting testimony. For many witnesses, it is a privilege and opportunity to appear before a congressional panel. It can mean publicity and exposure.

But Congress also has the power to subpoena witnesses and information. This means that a legal document is issued to ensure that witnesses comply with the committee's order. Committees may be granted judicial powers to charge individuals with contempt of Congress. They may also issue warrants for the arrest of such individuals.

Committees have an important role to play in monitoring federal government agencies (which are part of the executive branch). Again the government's system of checks and balances comes into play. Members of the president's cabinet, department heads, and agency officials are frequently summoned to testify before committees. For example, the secretary of defense might be called to testify regarding the need for advanced weaponry or research into satellite tracking systems. Committee meetings are also one of the arenas where special interest groups and lobbyists exert their influence.

Senate committees set up hearings to approve federal department head appointments, Supreme Court nominees, and the appointment of the president's cabinet members.

In recent years, committee hearings that deal with investigations have tended to become media events. Camera operators and news teams have become as commonplace in the committee room as witnesses testifying before committee members. In 1991, when Clarence Thomas was nominated to the Supreme Court, it was a Senate committee that interviewed the experienced judge regarding—among other items—his alleged sexual harassment of Anita Hill and other women employees who had worked for him. Newspaper headlines and broadcast news segments keep the world informed of some of the proceedings in committee rooms. C-SPAN, the twenty-four-hour congressional cable TV network, and other TV stations sometimes air hours of such testimony.

☆ ══════════ ☆

Senator Joseph Biden, chairman of the Senate Judiciary Committee, huddled with other members of the committee after the voting on the nomination of Clarence Thomas to the Supreme Court in 1991. Senator Strom Thurmond, ranking Republican of the committee, is seated on his right.

☆ ════════ ☆

Senator Sam Ervin proved to be a
tenacious questioner as chairman of
the Senate Watergate Committee.

THE WATERGATE HEARINGS

In 1973 the Senate began to investigate an event that came to be known as the Watergate scandal. In the summer of 1972, several members of the committee to reelect Richard M. Nixon as president broke into the Democratic national headquarters at the Watergate apartment/office complex in Washington, D.C. Many of the key people involved in the initial break-in (and in the attempt to cover up the crime) were close associates of President Nixon. After news of the affair broke, Congress set up a special investigating committee to determine exactly how closely connected Nixon was to the burglary. The congressional committee was chaired by the colorful senator from North Carolina, Sam Ervin. Many of the committee's sessions were

A START IN POLITICS

Interestingly enough, one of the staff members on the Senate committee investigating Watergate was a young woman who had just graduated from Yale Law School. Her name? Hillary Rodham. The young lawyer later married a rising politician named Bill Clinton. In 1992 she became First Lady Hillary Rodham Clinton.

shown nationwide on TV, and Americans were fascinated and repelled by the deeds uncovered by the Senate's investigations.

At the same time, the House Judiciary Committee had uncovered enough evidence against President Nixon that a charge of impeachment (a formal accusation of wrongdoing against a public official) was about to be brought against the president. The committee felt that Nixon was wrong on three counts: "obstruction of justice, abuse of presidential power, and refusal to obey House subpoenas," according to Bruce Ragsdale in *The House of Representatives*.[2] It appeared that the president had known about the break-in, if not before it occurred, then soon thereafter. For a few weeks, the president's personal secretary, Rose Mary Woods, had shared the spotlight as she revealed how important sections of the president's taped telephone conversations had "accidentally" been erased.

But before the committee's findings could be brought before the full House for an impeachment vote, Nixon made an important decision. He did not want to face formal charges, and in August 1974 he became the first president to resign the office.

A LAW IS BORN

After considering all facets of a bill originated in the Senate, the committee then reports. If the committee disapproves, the bill dies. If not, the bill goes to the full Senate for approval. Any senators who still disapprove can further delay consent of the bill.

If the bill is approved by the Senate, it then goes to the House, where a similar journey begins. If the House fails to pass the bill, it goes back to the Senate. There it may be further debated and undergo more revisions. If the bill shows promise, a conference committee may be set up to bring both sides into agreement. Sometimes a compromise can be reached, but sometimes not. Both sides may give in on a few of their demands in order to reach an agreement.

If, finally, the Senate and House both approve the bill, it goes to the president for his signature. If the president signs it, the bill then becomes a law.

FOUR
CONGRESS AND THE COMMITTEE STRUCTURE

For members of Congress, serving on a committee—and especially the "right" committee—is a matter of extreme importance. The most significant committees draw the politically ambitious. Committee work gives members of Congress much of their identity, and reputations can often be forged by accomplishments made as a member of a committee.

Committees give lesser-known senators the chance to be heard and also to develop their political skills. Committee work also broadens the careers of many senators and allows them to delve into areas outside their usual realm of experience. Being asked to serve on a particular committee can make a career. Helping the member's constituents back home is the bottom line, the measure of how effectively the member is serving and representing those who elected him or her. Subcommittee work, too, can be important, especially for junior members.

GETTING ON A COMMITTEE

Prior to the opening session of a new Congress, newly elected members are asked to name their preferences for committee assignments. Membership on the various committees is divided between the two major political parties in proportion to their membership in the House or Senate. At the start of a typical congressional session in recent years, almost two-thirds of freshman representatives were assigned to the committees of their first choice.

To the extent possible, the committees of each house try to

honor requests for seats on them, but there are many constraints that limit their flexibility in this respect. Party ratios dictate the numbers of Democrats and Republicans who can be seated on any particular committee. Democrats in the House consider membership on any one of the three special committees—Rules, Appropriations, and Ways and Means—to be "exclusive." In other words, a member who serves on one of these committees cannot serve on any other standing committee.

According to party rules, House Democrats may serve on no more than five subcommittees. House Republicans do not have such stringent rules, although it is unusual for a Republican who has a choice or "blue-ribbon" assignment to serve on any other committee.

HOW PARTY MEMBERSHIP IMPACTS COMMITTEE ASSIGNMENTS

In the House, both Democratic and Republican members form their own ad hoc Committee of Committees, which oversees the placement of party members on congressional committees. At the beginning of a session of Congress, caucuses of Democrats and Republicans elect committee members. The majority party furnishes the majority of committee members.

Republican senators are assigned their committee position by the Senate Committee of Committees, made up of senior Republican senators (those who have served at least one Senate term). The Senate Democratic Steering Committee gives Democratic senators their committee assignments. Typically a senator will serve on two standing committees as well as several select committees. The majority party sees that the majority party members control each committee—at least numerically.

The majority party elects the Speaker of the House and controls the House Rules Committee. It also—through an ad hoc Steering and Policy Committee—appoints all committee and subcommittee chairpersons. The majority-controlled Rules Committee oversees bills that make it to the floor for discussion and debate, seeing that proper legislative procedures are followed.

Seniority—the number of years of service in Congress—is a chief factor in appointing both chairpersons and members to important committee and subcommittee posts. Often, simply by exhibiting the required staying power, members of Congress can advance over time to powerful positions. Seniority also governs where members of Congress are seated within their respective chambers.

The presiding officers of the Senate and House personally appoint members to special or select committees. To do this, they rely heavily on the recommendations of standing committee members. These are usually veteran politicians whom the presiding officers have known and worked with for years.

Special interest groups (lobbies) often take an intense interest in committee memberships and may lobby on behalf of specific appointments. Political action committees (PACs) often enter the fray as well. PACs are frequently the money-dispensing arms of particular lobbies. Congressional committees often try to do what these special interests want in order to safeguard political contributions. Lobbies and PACs can be powerful persuaders, especially when major contributions to party campaign funds are at stake. From the congressional perspective, such politically based appointments can have major impact. For example, if a member who favors foreign aid is named to the Appropriations Committee, foreign aid will end up being a priority on the committee's agenda.

COMMITTEE MEMBERSHIP

A member of Congress may have many reasons for wanting to serve on a particular committee. Among these reasons could be the desire to advance a career, a plan to help constituents (who may be either the voters at home or lobbyists), and a need to achieve power and/or political leverage—the ability to garner votes within Congress and support through the system of favors and mutual support that underlies so much of the action of Congress.

There are many outside forces that work upon legislators, such as pressure groups, lobbyists, PACs, constituencies, petitions, et cetera. Committees, on the other hand, are an important internal force. Legislators who have not made up their own mind on an issue often turn to their colleagues and friends in Congress to see how they are voting. Studies have repeatedly shown that members of Congress take their cues from other members whose opinions they respect more than from any other source.[1] If the respected colleague is a member of the relevant committee, the colleague's opinions (and votes) are that much more persuasive. In fact, at least one study has shown that constituency needs are the least important factor in the decision-making process working on members of Congress.[2]

As William Ashworth points out, "Almost universally, the lion's share of the spending of any federal agency ends up going to the states of the senators and representatives . . . who are members of the committees which oversee the affairs of that particular agency."[3] This inequity can vary, with the average per capita spending often two or more times greater for those states whose senators or representatives are members of the appropriate committee.

Gaining a coveted assignment requires a personal public relations campaign on the part of the committee hopeful. This campaign will involve speaking with steering committee members who will make the assignment, displaying any relevant credentials and generally playing the game of politics. Switching committee assignments requires much the same strategy.

There is more than enough committee work to go around. Most legislators serve on a number of committees—standing, select, and others. On average, members of the House of Representatives sit on about six committees, while senators serve on almost twice that number. These multiple assignments come about largely through serving on a number of subcommittees.

COMMITTEE CHAIRS

The center of power of a given committee is determined mostly by its chair. The committee chairperson is always a member of the majority party. The chairperson's particular leadership style largely determines the character of the committee and how smoothly it functions. Some committee chairs exercise an iron hand over their committees. Even though subcommittees may exist in theory, the chair may render them virtually powerless by insisting that most issues be dealt with in full committee. Politically conservative chairwomen and chairmen generally keep a tight rein on the activities of the subcommittees under their control.

Chairs appoint subcommittees and determine their party ratios. They refer specific bills to subcommittees for consideration. Committee chairs manage their committees' schedules and serve as "floor managers," guiding bills through deliberations.

The chair also presides over meetings of the full committee, sets up times for committee meetings, and reports on committee findings to the full House or Senate. Finally, the committee chair also makes recommendations on appointments to the conference committees that hammer out the differences between the House and Senate views on specific pieces of legislation.

STAFFS AND FUNDING

Among the chair's duties are to approve committee and subcommittee members' expenses and to oversee all other expenditures. Chairs recruit and fix salaries for professional staff. This is an important job, since committees employ sizable staffs. Each committee staff numbers at least fifty to sixty people who assist Congress members in their work. The Senate alone has a support staff of more than 7,000 employees. This is roughly seventy staffers for each senator.

In general, Senate committees seem to require the largest staffs. The House formed a permanent Select Committee on

Intelligence in 1974 to oversee the work of the U.S. intelligence community. An equivalent Senate committee was formed in 1975. This was in response to the perceived abuses by intelligence gathering activities during the Nixon administration. Within five years, members of the House committee had employed a staff of twenty-four, while Senate members could get by with no fewer than forty-five staff members, nearly twice as many.[4]

Committee funds are often spent on hearings outside Washington. These "field hearings" are on-site investigations that take place wherever is most appropriate. Fact-finding missions may involve travel abroad by committee and staff members. For example, members of the committee deciding foreign aid appropriations may travel to the Middle East or to other global hot spots. Congressional committees also spend money to pay the expenses of bringing in experts to provide testimony.

Statutes limit the basic size of standing committee staffs and the cost of running them. However, committees circumvent these limitations by annually voting extra funds for "investigations and inquiries" to committees that request additional monies. New committees, select committees, task forces, caucuses, and study groups are constantly forming and re-forming, requiring staff appointments and new funding appropriations.

The size of a committee's staff and/or budget seems to be unrelated to that committee's effectiveness. Large staffs are not necessarily unwieldy, wasteful, and inefficient. Sometimes committees with enormous staffs are, surprisingly, models of efficiency, while some smaller committee staffs (lean is not always mean) seem incapable of addressing the business at hand. Evaluations of committee and staff effectiveness must be made on a case-by-case basis.

FIVE
A LOOK AT SOME SPECIFIC COMMITTEES

In general, the most desirable committee choices are those concerned *directly* with money. These include the House and Senate committees devoted to the budget, taxation, and appropriations.

Membership on the House Energy and Commerce Committee is also eagerly sought. This committee covers such a broad spectrum of endeavors, ranging from trade and transportation to professional sports teams and regulation of oil refineries, that members may exert influence over many different government agencies and/or business enterprises. Because of these wide-ranging powers, committee members are often targeted by different political action committees (PACs) that have money to contribute to campaign coffers.

THE BIG FOUR

The committees with the most power are those that hold the country's purse strings. Two of them belong to the House of Representatives—the House Ways and Means Committee and the House Appropriations Committee, while two belong to the Senate—the Senate Finance Committee and the Senate Appropriations Committee. These committees control the revenue system for the entire nation and they see how every penny of that money is spent.

The percentages seesaw from year to year, but it is not unusual for any one of these four major financial committees to control between 25 and 40 percent of all federal government expenditures during any given year.[1] This means that relatively small groups of a few dozen people each have tremendous concentrations of power as they determine how hundreds of billions of tax dollars will be spent.

Members of Congress consider these committees the choicest appointments. The senior members who control committee membership selection exercise a careful screening process. They frequently ask questions about prospective members' positions on many topics. Do they favor or oppose agriculture and other industries? What is their position on subsidies (grants) to the tobacco industry? Do they want to consider special allowances to oil companies, "pork barrel" appropriations, or any of a hundred other topics? The committee room often becomes a battleground between liberal and conservative interests. In general, in a conservative Congress those with liberal leanings may have to forget about being welcomed on one of these committees, and vice versa.

For members of Congress, sitting on the "right" committee can mean the difference between a political career that goes nowhere and one that can bring decades of influence on a national scale. It can also be a stop on the road to the White House. In recent history, Richard Nixon's fast political rise can easily be traced to his committee work (see page 47).

SENATE APPROPRIATIONS COMMITTEE

The U.S. Senate Appropriations Committee is one of the most powerful committees in Congress. Its members have a direct and continuing impact on *every* program administered by the federal government. An analysis of how many times each state has been represented on the Appropriations Committee over the past century reveals interesting disparities. One study showed Arizona had seated members on the committee more than three times as often as New York, Pennsylvania, or Connecticut—states regarded as highly visible, socially important, and politically active.[2] Western states have fared somewhat better than the East in securing representation. It may be that senators from the

West have more aggressively campaigned for positions on the powerful committee. Coupled with their constituents' demands, ranging from military bases to irrigation projects and hydroelectric dams, such disproportionate representation has helped lead to the West's phenomenal economic growth and (some might say) to the East's decline.

THE HOUSE WAYS AND MEANS COMMITTEE

The House Ways and Means Committee considers all legislation that concerns taxes. This committee holds hearings and listens to testimony from many kinds of experts as well as from members of the public and representatives of businesses—the people who

Representative Daniel Rostenkowski (D-Ill.), chairperson of the House Ways and Means Committee, and Senator Robert Packwood (R-Ore.), chairperson of the Senate Finance Committee, used World War I army helmets to signify their anticipated long stay in the trenches over the tax bill in 1986.

will have to pay the taxes. Committee members ask these people questions and listen to the arguments for and against the new legislation. After discussing the good and bad points, they decide how to act upon each bill.

A decision to raise the taxes on gasoline might involve months of testimony by financial experts, chemists, car manufacturers and dealers, service station owners, and consumers from all over the country. Before laws are enacted, Congress tries to assess what impact the legislation will have on the economy, on tax revenues, on the environment, and on the everyday life of citizens.

BUDGET COMMITTEES

The Budget Committees that operate in both the House and the Senate do not have much real legislative power. They function broadly to set goals and targets and to establish spending priorities for those committees such as Appropriations that oversee exactly how government monies are spent. Members of the Budget Committees are among the first to review the president's proposed budget each year. Their assessment of the president's recommendations has a direct influence on setting guidelines for the actual budget that Congress will eventually approve.

The Budget Committees act as a conscience for the committees that do the real spending. They are the chief watchdogs under the Gramm Rudman Hollings Act, passed in 1985, which set the goal—not yet achieved—of working toward deficit reduction and a balanced budget.

RULES COMMITTEE

The House Rules Committee has tremendous influence on legislation but no power over federal spending. Every major bill has to pass through the Rules Committee before it can be debated on the House floor. The Rules Committee also controls the order in which bills are acted upon in the House and limits the amount of time that can be devoted to debate. The committee has the authority to oversee all debate of the bill. In this way, the Rules Committee has the potential to challenge, delay, or limit almost any piece of legislation.

SELECT COMMITTEE ON ETHICS

The Constitution requires that Congress discipline itself. This precedent was established not to grant legislators an immunity to prosecution—to create a privileged class of lawmakers who are themselves somehow above the law—but to free them from unnecessary interference by the judicial and executive branches.

Rules governing the makeup of the Select Committee on Ethics call for a balance of freshman members, members in their second term, and senior members—those who have completed two terms or more of congressional service. The Senate regularly seats six members on the Ethics Committee, while the House sends a twelve-member panel.

Ethics code reforms initiated under the Carter administration in 1978 included requirements for members of the House and Senate to disclose their financial worth. The reforms also imposed guidelines on income earned from sources outside Congress. A secret operation by the FBI conducted in 1980 called Abscam uncovered several instances of serious misconduct by members of Congress, leading to resignations, expulsions, and even convictions. The types of misdoings uncovered included shady property transactions, double billing on expense accounts, misuse of government property, and misappropriations of campaign funds. The press and law enforcement officials have increasingly become interested in the legal and ethical lapses of members of Congress. Many instances of bribery, sexual misconduct, and fraud have come to light in recent years.

Many would say that Congress has been lax about keeping its members in line. It is often difficult to find members who are enthusiastic about sitting on the Ethics Committee. Sometimes members feel constrained about censuring their colleagues. They may also feel that if they overlook faults in others, no one will call attention to their own shortcomings. Also, a false accusation or other wrong move at the wrong time can spell political death.

THE MOST NOTORIOUS COMMITTEE OF ALL

Established in the 1930s, the House Un-American Activities Committee (HUAC) was the creation of the all-but-forgotten Representative Samuel Dickstein. The intent of the committee was to investigate questionable actions and individuals. In effect, though, the committee reached its full power in the 1940s post-war period, when it began to "expose" people and actions it defined as subversive.

In the late 1940s, Alger Hiss, Whittaker Chambers, and Elizabeth Bentley were all subpoenaed to appear before the committee. They were all people who, it was believed, either were communists in the period before World War II or had links to the American Communist Party. Hiss testified that he had no prior knowledge of Chambers; later this was found to be untrue, and Hiss was accused of having lied under oath.

The committee began to have a really powerful impact on Americans beginning in the early 1950s. Under the guidance of Senator Joseph R. McCarthy, HUAC began to question citizens about their involvement with the Communist Party. This was a time shortly after World War II when the Soviets were expanding their domination over people and countries, mostly in Eastern Europe. Many people felt that any connection with or even interest in things relating to the Soviet Union put one under suspicion. They also felt that any connection with the Communist Party was definitely un-American and bordered on treason.

Writers, scientists, and performers, among others, were called before the committee to testify about their political beliefs, both past and present. Almost anyone who had ever even flirted with socialism or who had any ties to any communist sympathizers was fair game for interrogation.

☆ ══════ ☆

In December 1948, Representative Richard M. Nixon (R-Cal.)
views microfilm, with Robert L. Stripling, chief investigator
for HUAC. The films were found on the Maryland farm
of Whittaker Chambers, an admitted former Soviet agent.

A question asked of most of these witnesses that was to echo throughout the committee hearings was, "Are you now, or have you ever been, a member of the Communist Party?" The whole communist witch-hunt was a reaction to the nation's cold war with the Soviet Union. But soon the country's zealous guarding of patriotism began to backfire. Many lives and reputations were permanently damaged, and some of the witnesses were blacklisted in their professions, never to practice their crafts again. The televised hearings were broadcast to the nation and brought ruin to many creative people's reputations.

American feelings changed dramatically over sixteen months. By December of 1954, McCarthy was censured (officially and publicly criticized) by the Senate for his behavior, and his political career was over. Ironically, he, too, was no longer able to work in his chosen field, having brought shame to himself and to much of the American government.

A young Republican senator from California named Richard M. Nixon became a key player in the HUAC testimonies. Nixon's rise is one of the best modern examples of how a young politician's budding career can be boosted by serving on a congressional committee.

ACTRESS UNDER SUSPICION

Even Nancy Davis (later to become Mrs. Ronald Reagan, First Lady of one of our most popular presidents) was questioned by HUAC. It turned out, in fact, that the Miss Davis the committee was looking for was another actress with the same name.

SIX

WHAT DO THE HEADLINES MEAN?

The 1990s have been a particularly active period for Congress's committees as American lawmakers have considered new policies and programs and legislative agendas that will have a lasting impact on the nation's well-being, especially as it heads into the twenty-first century. Important decisions regarding fiscal policy, health care reform, and additional funding to fight crime in our nation's cities are all part of the current committee agenda.

In July of 1994, Federal Reserve chairman Alan Greenspan testified in front of the Senate Banking, Housing, and Urban Affairs Committee regarding the state of the nation's economic health. His assessment, and his decision on whether to raise interest rates to head off inflation, can have a major impact on every aspect of the country's economy—from the mortgage rates that home owners pay to the availability of funds for business expansion to the income that retirees receive from investments.

More and more, the internal workings of committees in Congress are gaining a higher profile in the daily news media. The public is able to get a clearer sense of how discussions in the committee room affect the laws passed in Congress and, ultimately, the way the government impacts their lives. Because congressional committees decide what laws will be passed and what programs the government will undertake, this can translate into which segments of the workforce will have jobs and which will be unemployed.

THE BREYER CONFIRMATION

Hearings to confirm Stephen G. Breyer's appointment to the Supreme Court began in Washington, D.C., on July 12, 1994. Named by President Bill Clinton as his choice to succeed Justice Harry A. Blackmun on the nation's highest court, Breyer appeared before members of the Senate Judiciary Committee. This committee is authorized to investigate and determine whether or not a person is suitable to sit on the bench of the nation's highest federal court. Through several days of testimony, Breyer calmly answered the questions put to him by members of the committee.

The eighteen-member committee was composed of ten Democrats and eight Republicans. Questions about Breyer's stands on abortion and the death penalty were posed by the committee. An article in the *New York Times* stated Breyer was "a cautious nominee . . . keeping most answers at a level of generality that guarded against expressing a view on issues that might come before the Court."[1]

On July 16, 1994, Neil A. Lewis wrote in the *New York Times*, "The hearing that ended today showed how much the confirmation process has changed over the years. Until 1929 the Senate acted on all nominations without questioning the nominee. It was not until 1939, when Felix Frankfurter was nominated by President Franklin D. Roosevelt, that the Judiciary Committee began the practice of questioning nominees."[2] One of the unique aspects of the Frankfurter nomination was that he was Jewish. The Senate committee members of that time felt that they really had to prove Frankfurter's suitability for the post.

On July 19, 1994 Breyer's nomination was unanimously approved by the Senate Judiciary Committee. Ten days later, the findings of the committee went before the full Senate, and Breyer was easily confirmed as a new Supreme Court justice.

☆ ══════ ☆

Senator Edward Kennedy (D-Mass.) and Senator James Jeffords (R-Vt.)
meet with Charleston, South Carolina, Mayor Joseph Riley Jr.
prior to a hearing on arts funding before the Senate Labor Committee
in February 1995. Actor Christopher Reeve, co-president
of the Creative Coalition, (second from right) looks on.

ARTS FUND CUTS

The arts in America have always been on shaky ground, particularly when it comes to government funding. Corporations and private foundations often underwrite the costs of many musical and theater events, but it is becoming increasingly difficult to find resources from the federal government for any kind of arts subsidies.

The situation worsened in July of 1994 when the Senate Appropriations Committee recommended a 5 percent cut in the budget for the National Endowment for the Arts (NEA).

This amounts to a cut of $8.5 million from an overall budget of just $170 million. Spending of public money to support arts events lags behind the level of spending found in most developed countries.

Often such cutbacks result from constituents' unhappiness over the way that public money is being spent. Sometimes people are offended by what they see as public support for "indecent" performances or art exhibitions. In 1991 the NEA was accused of squandering taxpayers' money when a grant from the organization sponsored an exhibition of nude photographs by controversial photographer Robert Mapplethorpe. Some people considered the display obscene. When those who were offended made themselves known, committee members were forced to take their complaints seriously.

HEALTH REFORM

One of the country's most important measures ever—providing health care insurance for the entire American population—was debated over much of an extended congressional session in the summer of 1994.

In the fall of 1993, Clinton introduced his proposed health care reform program as a bill in Congress. In March of 1994, the House Ways and Means Subcommittee concluded that there was a need for overhauling the health care system. Three committees adopted the bill, along with the president's demands that health care coverage be universal and that employers foot the bill for all the insurance.

But by midsummer, Congress could not agree on those terms. The Senate Finance Committee suggested universal coverage, but not until the year 2002, and the committee did not feel that employers should pay most of the costs.

Largely the bill came unglued because of party differences. Party lines have gotten in the way of political action. *Time* magazine reported, "After Democrats in the House Ways and Means Committee tried to build a coalition with tax cuts and other sweeteners, House minority whip [Republican] Newt Gingrich told colleagues to vote against amendments designed to broaden support for reform."[3] Many felt that Democrats bent over backward to answer the initial objections of Republicans to the health plan, but Republicans refused to lend their support and the bill died. Despite the failure to get the bill enacted into law, the issue of public health care reform is one that will not go away.

THE CRIME BILL

Another disappointment for President Bill Clinton came in the summer of 1994, when his much-vaunted crime bill was initially turned down by the House, in a 225 to 210 defeat. A great deal of the problem was concerned with the enormous budget: $30.2 billion. While most of the money was for straightforward spending, the bill got stuck on such tricky issues as gun control and capital punishment. *Time* magazine reported that it seemed to many in Congress who voted no that too much of the huge amount of money was targeted for "pork barrel" measures that "included too many social-work incentives for activities such as midnight basketball and self-esteem counseling for inner-city kids."[4]

Also, there are many people who feel that the responsibility for making laws regarding crime in the cities should not properly rest with the federal government, but with state and local governments. Interestingly, both *Newsweek* and *U.S. News & World Report* devoted the cover articles of their August 15, 1994, issues to the problems of rising crime. Both are weekly news magazines with enormous nationwide circulation.

As with the health reform bill, many House members split, with Democrats voting for the bill and Republicans voting against it, a good example of partisan gridlock. But according to *Time*, even some staunch Democrats—Clinton's followers—"jumped ship."[5] That was on the first vote. The bill later passed in both houses of Congress and was signed into law by President Clinton.

Congressional committees are incredibly powerful. The Senate oversees appointments to the nation's highest court. Committee decisions may determine who has health insurance and who does not, whether extra tax monies will be applied to fighting crime, or whether the president maintains credibility. The actions that committees take, the bills that they pass or do not pass, have a direct bearing on the daily lives of the more than 260 million people who live in this country.

STANDING SENATE COMMITTEES (AS OF 1994)

Agriculture, Nutrition, and Forestry
Appropriations
Armed Services
Banking, Housing, and Urban Affairs
Budget
Commerce, Science, and Transportation
Energy and Natural Resources
Environment and Public Works
Finance
Foreign Relations
Governmental Affairs
Judiciary
Labor and Human Resources
Rules and Administration
Small Business
Veterans' Affairs

STANDING HOUSE COMMITTEES (AS OF 1994)
☆

Agriculture
Appropriations
Armed Services
Banking, Finance, and Urban Affairs
Budget
District of Columbia
Education and Labor
Energy and Commerce
Foreign Affairs
Government Operations
House Administration
Judiciary
Merchant Marine and Fisheries
Natural Resources
Post Office and Civil Service
Public Works and Transportation
Rules
Science, Space, and Technology
Small Business
Standards of Official Conduct
Veterans' Affairs
Ways and Means

SOURCE NOTES

Introduction

1. Mark Green, *Who Runs Congress?*, 3d ed. (New York: Bantam Books, 1979), 61.

One

1. Bruce A. Ragsdale, *The House of Representatives* (New York: Chelsea House, 1989), 36.

Two

1. Abner J. Mikva and Patti B. Saris, *The American Congress: The First Branch* (New York: Franklin Watts, 1983), 242.

Three

1. Donald A. Ritchie. *The Senate* (New York: Chelsea House, 1988), 74.

2. Ragsdale, *The House of Representatives*, 60.

Four

1. Malcolm E. Jewell and Samuel C. Patterson, *The Legislative Process in the United States*, 4th ed. (New York: Random House, 1986), 88.

2. Ibid., 89.

3. William Ashworth, *Under the Influence: Congress, Lobbies, and the American Pork-Barrel System* (New York: Hawthorn and Dutton, 1983), 22.

4. Harrison W. Fox, Jr., and Susan Webb Hammond, *The Congressional Staffs* (New York: Free Press, 1977), 24.

Five

1. *Power in Congress: Who Has It, How They Got It, How They Use It* (Washington, D.C.: Congressional Quarterly, 1987), 60.

2. Steven S. Smith and Christopher J. Deering, *Committees in Congress* (Washington, D.C.: CQ Press, 1984), 117.

Six

1. Neil A. Lewis, "Taking Initiative, Nominee Defends Conduct as Judge," *New York Times*, July 13, 1994, Section A.

2. Neil A. Lewis, "Breyer Has Opportunity to Recount His Story," *New York Times*, July 16, 1994, Section A.

3. "Health Care: Breaking a Promise," *Time*, June 27, 1994, 41.

4. *Time*, August 22, 1994, 38.

5. Ibid.

ad hoc temporary committee, arising out of a particular need at a particular time.

appropriations money designated for a particular purpose.

bill a proposed piece of legislation.

bipartisan having members from both major political parties.

budget a plan for spending money.

caucus a particular interest group made up of individuals from within the larger legislative body, as the women's caucus and the Democratic caucus.

censure official criticism, ranging from a reprimand to serious criminal charges, directed at a member of Congress.

coalition members of diverse groups who join together to show their agreement on a certain issue.

compromise a mutually acceptable decision reached between two different groups.

conference committee an ad hoc joint committee that hammers out differences between the House and Senate versions of a bill to be voted upon.

constituents the voters and residents of a member of Congress's district.

in committee said of bills when under consideration by a congressional committee.

joint committees committees with members from both the House of Representatives and the Senate.

jurisdiction a specific and defined area of interest covered by a particular committee.

negotiations discussions that attempt to arrive at an agreement.

permanent committees see *standing committees.*

pork barrel money appropriated for projects of limited and usually regional interest. The term is derogatory and describes "fat" or waste in the budget.

proposal a suggested policy measure or piece of legislation to be considered.

revenue money received by the government through taxes, fees, and other sources.

select committees also known as special committees. Temporary committees set up to consider a specific problem or concern. They may exist for a period of months or years.

standing committees permanent, lasting committees set up to deal with particular types of legislation. Membership may change, but the committee goes on year after year.

subcommittees smaller, "task force" committees made up of limited numbers of members of a standing committee assigned to study a particular issue.

FURTHER READING

Ashworth, William. *Under the Influence: Congress, Lobbies, and the American Pork-Barrel System.* New York: Hawthorn and Dutton, 1983.

Goodman, Walter. *The Committee: The Extraordinary Career of the House Committee on Un-American Activities.* New York: Farrar, Straus & Giroux, 1968.

Jewell, Malcolm E., and Samuel C. Patterson. *The Legislative Process in the United States.* 4th ed. New York: Random House, 1986.

Meltzer, Milton. *American Politics: How It Really Works.* New York: Morrow Junior Books, 1989.

Mikva, Abner J., and Patti B. Saris. *The American Congress: The First Branch.* New York: Franklin Watts, 1983.

Power in Congress: Who Has It, How They Got It, How They Use It. Washington D.C.: Congressional Quarterly, 1987.

Ragsdale, Bruce A. *The House of Representatives.* New York: Chelsea House, 1989.

Ritchie, Donald A. *The Senate.* New York: Chelsea House, 1988.

Smith, Steven S., and Christopher J. Deering. *Committees in Congress.* Washington, D.C.: CQ Press, 1984.

ABOUT THE AUTHOR

Cass R. Sandak is the author of more than fifty nonfiction books for children. He has written about the sciences, sports, holidays, exploration and civilization, and politics. He has also written many biographies and articles on a variety of topics. His books have been cited by the British Trust for Children's Literature and the National Association for the Advancement of Science.

The author graduated summa cum laude from Union College in Schenectady, New York, and did graduate work at the University of Pennsylvania. For several years he has been a consultant in technical, scientific, and promotional writing for corporate clients. He is a member of Phi Beta Kappa and the Academy of American Poets.

Mr. Sandak divides his time between New York City and home in upstate New York. In his free moments, he enjoys traveling and is active in community affairs.